Snapshots of Jesus

In her latest work, "Snapshot of Jesus Through the Lens of History", I see the same "Voice for Love" and clear guidance that Bette Jean uses in her other works, the Voice that seems beyond the conceptual mind, yet allows us to see and understand. The loving light Bette Jean shines upon all she does is demonstrated in this new book. By portraying the historical Jesus in his daily life experiences, we are called to enter into an intimate relationship with our elder brother.

I first met Bette Jean Cundiff in 1980 at the 1st East Coast 'A Course in Miracles' Conference, held at the Plaza Hotel in New York City. Bette Jean and her partner (the late Paul Steinberg) hosted the event. For me it was a day of new experiences, never to be forgotten which changed my life forever. For the first time since I began a study of 'A Course in Miracles', I recognized the help I asked for was there for me, so I could to go deeper in my understanding, That afternoon, we broke up into smaller circles and I was blessed to sit at Bette Jean's table. She used clear, gentle examples to clarify Course words I thought I "knew". She spoke of the mystical meanings these words held for serious Course students. The one word I didn't see necessary then was gratitude. Yet, 33 years later, I experience love and gratitude as one - gratitude for the peace of God that IS, always.

Through the years, Bette Jean Cundiff practiced the same passionate caring for all the projects she has been given to deliver to a whole generation of truth seekers. Her early guidance to provide "The Children's Material", a miracle course for young people, answered the call of parents worldwide who already found wisdom and comfort in the adult Course and wanted to share it with their children. Bette Jean's gift is to provide clarity in easy-to-understand terms, for what appears complex to the truth seeker.

Today at age of 73, I am grateful for having Bette Jean in my life so early on my path. Love is the way I walk in Gratitude, Bette Jean.

In Full Appreciation Always.

David Fishman

(New York, N.Y.)

Snapshots of Jesus - Through the Lens of History

Table of Contents

Where you will find each 'Snapshot'...

Snapshots of Jesus - Through the Lens of History

Wouldn't you like to jump in a time machine? - 10

Aiming the Lens Back in Time – 16

PART I   THE EARLY YEARS

Jesus – the Jewish Kid Next Door - 22

Nazareth – the 'sticks', the 'hood', the city? - 28

Jesus – Nerd or Bad Boy? Coming of Age - 34

Jesus – the Invisible - 40

The Cousins John and Jesus - 44

Still Willing to Go Exploring? - 48

Teen-age Reels Finding a Cause –
          John and Jesus - 52

PART II   THE WORK BEGINS

John the Prophet of Doom - 58

Baptism, Purity and the 'Morning Dippers' - 62

The Political Minefield Jesus Enters - 66

The Good the Bad the Ugly:
Essenes, Sadducees, Pharisees and Bandits - 70

Apocalypse Now? Prophecy? Policy?
          . . .should I prepare? - 74

The Dead Sea Scrolls and the Essenes - 80

Snapshots of Jesus - Through the Lens of History

Did Jesus go to India and Tibet? - 86

Abracadabra, Jesus and Kabbalah - 92

Time for Intention - 96

Will the real Jesus please stand up? - 100

The Temptations - 106

How do you define Messiah? Ha! You'd be surprised. - 110

Jesus and His Handlers - 1116

Radical and Beyond - 120

'Saturday Night Live' with Jesus on the Mountain – 124

Doctor Jesus – 128

THE LAST WEEK

The Passover Powder Keg - 134

Dinner for thirteen, please. - 140

In the Garden - 144

Trial by Sanhedrin - 148

Pontius Pilate – A Day at the Office - 152

The Crucifixion - 158

Aftermath – Splinters - 164

Resurrection – A Very Private Matter - 170

INTRODUCTION

Snapshots of Jesus - Through the Lens of History

Wouldn't you like to jump into a time machine...

Snapshots of Jesus - Through the Lens of History

Wouldn't you like to jump into a time machine and be back for even one hour in a time and place you always wondered about? Isn't that why we so enjoy history based movies that are exquisitely designed, filmed and directed to thrust us emotionally and visually into another life and time period?

In high school I attended a history class that covered the ancient world and my mind lit up so brightly I was sure everyone could see the glow. I was fascinated! I was hooked! Though I have grown to love history in general, the ancient world is the one that captures my heart and mind the most explosively.

Later, when an adult and student of 'A Course in Miracles' I happily morphed into a world speaker and shared my growing insight about the Course with thousands of other students around the world. Naturally, my curiosity about comparative religions and philosophies blossomed and my personal library grew into the hundreds of learned works in this double field of religion and ancient history. I know that sounds impressive, but I have to admit, though I may be informed in these areas, I am definitely not a true scholar. Instead, like you I consider myself an armchair scholar armed with a laptop.

Though, over the thirties years of lecturing around the country I had gained a true closeness to the Jesus presented in 'A Course in Miracles', I now wanted to meet Him in His own time period. To do this I created this, my very own 'time machine' of study.

Hungrily I reviewed many of the books I already had and added several more including 'Josephus', the highly respected Jewish historian's books that he wrote during the early first century and the Archaeological Bible, filled with historical detail. Then, I added to my collection a DVD of the Frontline special 'From Jesus to Christ, The First Christians', a four hour special offering a wonderful modern look at Jesus by highly respected scholars. Finally, I connected through the internet to hundreds of articles by renowned scholars on the life and times of Jesus and the early Church.

I had my expanded armchair studies in place.

Since starting my project, I have been gaining eye opening understanding and would love to share it with you. So, following will be the 'snapshots' I have taken so you can virtually join me and travel back to the life and times of Jesus.

<u>Snapshots of Jesus - Through the Lens of History</u>

Grab your camera, take your own snapshots and start building an album of your own as you see Jesus through the lens of history come alive . . .

Preparing for My Photo Journey

Aiming the lens back in time. . .

Snapshots of Jesus - Through the Lens of History

Taking a look at Jesus in the present moment, while trying to see him as he was two thousand years ago, creates an immediate conflict. Let's use this phrase as an example: "taking its own sweet time". A city slicker like me might ask what does 'sweet time' have to do with the computer project I'm trying to complete in a timely manner? Yet, it wasn't until I moved into a country home with an honest to goodness vegetable garden, that I heard myself saying, "those green tomatoes will just be ready in their own sweet time", and the phrase actually meant what it said. I remember having one of those "Duh!" moments. A farmer coined that phrase a long time ago for his maturing fruits and vegetables. The phrase made sense in that context. Though often repeated today it is really just gobble gook for a townie.

Just think of modern slang, political

scandals and complaints, 'in' jokes and the growing distance between well written English and a teen's tweets. The mind boggles. Now, we begin to understand the gulf between understanding another culture, no less another time period. Understanding the 40s and 50s is hard enough—two thousand years is almost ridiculous. However, though surmounting this chasm is the first step in making sense of any 'snapshot' of the life and times of Jesus and will demand a whole bunch of research, I am officially retired. I have to admit the prospect sounds like fun.

And so I pile around me towers of books, bibles, articles, DVD's and set up an undemanding, yet consistent research schedule.

Whoa! Hold on! Two thousand years of cultural clutter, looking like a Hollywood reproduction of end world devastation clogs my lens view. Like a journalist/photographer in a war zone, I will have to wade carefully through the rebuilt and reconstructed, the hidden propaganda landmines of times past. Think of the overlays of New Age idealism, Victorian proprieties, bloody reformations and inquisitions, the burning of literature and sciences in the dark ages, the political imperatives and religious prejudices and superstitions all the way back to the bickering, backbiting and downright violent disagreements within the Jesus movement right from the get go in the first century. Whew!

Breathless, but still undaunted I make the commitment to continue. I shall don my suit of personal "body armor"—an open mind, the willingness to learn, to be wrong, to be disappointed and yes, to even be amazed!

...And I add one more piece of armor, perhaps the most important — my willingness to listen to the guidance of the Holy Spirit each step of the way.

PART I

The Early Years

Jesus - The Jewish Kid Next Door

Snapshots of Jesus - Through the Lens of History

Back in the day, when Jesus was young, he was just another kid running around with his brothers, sisters, cousins and friends in a small dusty town - repeat - another *Jewish* kid running around in a *Jewish* town. And that Jewish identity can't be underplayed. Jesus was immersed in his religious heritage every second of every day.

His Jewish family, like all others was large, extended and very close knit. Grandparents lived close by, as well as aunts and uncles. So a goodly number of Jesus' playmates were not only his siblings, but also first and second cousins. These were the relationships that would surround him, mold him and remain with him his whole life. He would go to one cousin for a ritual baptism, and others would join him as disciples.

His gang of playmates ran freely throughout the village and surrounding fields and farmlands. The natural world was an unending playground – a safe place without the fears modern parents harbor today. Family and friends were always close by.

Once a week Sabbath was observed and began at sun down. Jesus' mother, Mary, like all other wives and mothers would lead the family in prayer over that evening's meal. On the next morning, Jesus and his brothers would go with their Dad to the local synagogue.

Note, synagogues were meeting places in each village. In Jesus' day there was only one Temple – and that was in Jerusalem. On the Sabbath, the responsibility of all Dads became apparent. Boys were expected to be literate and able to read scripture aloud before the other men and their sons in the synagogue. Joseph, therefore, made sure to teach his sons Scripture, something that Jesus and his brothers probably had to study every day. Take note, however, another part of Jesus' training also occurred at this time. He and all the other boys learned to engage in what usually ended up being loud and emotionally charged debate on the meaning of scripture, not just between themselves, but with the learned men around them. Jews in the first century just loved 'in your face' discussion about everything – business, politics, and religion

And so from a very young age, Jesus with his brothers, cousins and friends struggled, studied and probably complained about their excellent regiment of study that included not just scripture but also the history of the Jewish nation and its culture. I can't help feeling that the fun part, however, was probably practicing the fine art of successful debate and argument among themselves and the adults around them.

This skill was to come in handy when the grown Jesus debated with the scribes who continually trailed behind and challenged him during his ministry. But, that will be covered in another snapshot.

. . .For now, we will leave this snapshot of the young Jesus, happily being just a kid.

Nazareth – the 'sticks', the 'hood', the city?

Snapshots of Jesus - Through the Lens of History

Let's zoom the lens back in time once more and take a quick shot of the town of Nazareth, the place where Jesus grew up. Will we find a small rural town out in the middle of nowhere? Or is it something else? Well, let's see what 'the hood' of Jesus' formative years was really like.

Picture a rural community of about five hundred people. Adobe homes, local market, a meeting place for a synagogue and Sabbath worship. Now walk barely fifteen feet beyond the houses and find the town circled by farms and vineyards. Sounds like what you expected, right? Let's take that first snapshot. But, wait. Let's open up the view lens wider and take another shot.

Just three miles north, a pleasant walk through the farms and vineyards, begins the sprawling, elegant, sophisticated Greco-Roman city of Sepphoris. Herod the Great's son, Herod Antipas began transforming the small town of Sepphoris, the birthplace of Jesus' mom Mary, into a virtual showplace. He started this ambitious project when Jesus was just a baby and by the time Jesus was grown it was not only one of the capital cities of the Galilee, but touted as the "Jewel of the Galilee" with requisite Roman aqua ducts, baths and amphitheatre, and all this seductive culture was just 'around the corner' from Nazareth.

Here was a city populated by moneyed Jews who were pro-Roman. The population included besides Jews, Romans, Greeks and various peoples from as far west as Egypt and beyond, and as far to the east as Persia and India. In fact, get this! The Romans had been importing silk from China for at least a hundred years already. The Silk Road was constantly being trampled. And Sepphoris was a crossroads through which much of this trade passed. How many languages where spoken? Definitely Greek, the language of trade, and also Aramaic, the common language of the surrounding Jewish population. Hebrew was fluently spoken in the synagogue by all Jews. The Roman rich and the Roman soldier would have spoken Latin. And then there would have been a smattering of all the other languages represented in this vibrant cosmopolitan city. In order to be able to function in the family business Jesus, like any member of this extended community had to have spoken and perhaps written at the very least Hebrew, Aramaic, and Greek, with a little bit of Latin thrown in.

The years of on-going building brought artisans into Sepphoris by the hundreds. This workforce was not made up of moneyed Jews, nor were they pro-Roman. This disgruntled group lived apart, outside the city, but within walking distance -- in towns just like Nazareth. Here our lens shows up the great divide, both financial and political. Just a mere three miles across farms and vineyards and we find to the south poor workers and farm laborers, and there just to the north 'within shouting distance' lived the land owners, the tax collectors and the 'rich and famous'. You can almost hear the complaints and grumbling in the south carrying over the fields into the homes of the snobs and conquerors to the north.

Jesus and his family lived as artisans, probably carpenters, to the south in Nazareth and commuted six days a week for years helping build the 'Jewel of the Galilee'. Carpenters would have been in great demand with guaranteed work for a lifetime. Joseph was well positioned to provide for his family and bring his sons into the family business. And every evening they walked home to their village after being subservient to the citizens of Sepphoris all day.

So what was Nazareth like, the small village where Jesus grew up? Here was a bedroom suburb filled with the poor workers and farm laborers, who supplied the needs of the rich and hated, and the conquerors and collaborators, next to a major Greco-Roman city and world crossroads. . .

. . . In other words, Nazareth was a small village of family, friends, spiritual support, and a hotbed of political unrest.

Jesus- Nerd or Bad Boy Coming of Age

As a kid in the fifties and sixties in Queens, New York, my own street was evenly divided among Protestants like me, Catholics and Jews. We played together as one big happy family – cops and robbers, cowboys and Indians, tag and stick ball. Then we all reached puberty at about the same time, and each of us was confirmed or had a bar/bat mitzvah and was recognized as an adult by our religious communities. We had giddily become teens while at the same time our parents watched and probably trembled with fear.

Now, let's go way back in time and take a snapshot of how a young Jew, like Jesus, marked his puberty and became a man in his religious community.

Dads had the responsibility to educate their sons in the Jewish tradition. Shortly after a boy's birth he was circumcised to mark him as a Jew. By five years old a boy was studying the Scripture, by ten years old he was studying the oral traditions. At twelve he would need to fast for the first time on the Day of Atonement to prepare himself for the year ahead when he would regularly sit at the feet of his rabbis, or teachers, learning and animatedly discussing theology. At thirteen he would now have studied the commandments, the Scriptures, the traditions and be ready for his big day when he was no longer a responsibility of his Dad, but now of his rabbis. He would legally become a man.

Keep in mind that there were three big Jewish holiday feasts that the male Jews (accompanied by their families – read that women and girl children) were required to attend at the only Temple in Jerusalem. Since attending three feasts a year was sometimes a burden, the pressure was placed on men to attend at least Passover once a year at the Temple. And here would be the perfect time for Joseph to take the twelve year old Jesus, so the boy could officially begin his studies with the rabbis. Jesus could now show his stuff and his readiness for becoming a man a year from then. This event was remembered by Mary and you can find it retold in the Gospel of Luke.

So, in Jesus' twelfth year, he accompanies his family on the yearly pilgrimage to Jerusalem for Passover. They join. the crowds and the hustle and bustle of thousands of Jews massing into Jerusalem for the Passover week. Let's take a quick snapshot of their destination, the Temple, and notice the acres and acres of courtyard inside the Temple complex. Over there are corrals filled with squealing lambs ready to be bought and then sacrificed for the holiday. Over here are the male members of extended families guffawing and slapping backs as they meet up after months of separation. And here and there we see small groups of rabbis loudly debating the intricacies of Jewish

LawThe noise must have been ear numbing.

Now zooming in we capture another shot. We see Jesus, a twelve years old boy, already eloquent, funny, really smart and utterly captivating. He has captured his audience of rabbis, and we can see them leaning forward, stroking their beards with intense interest in what this precocious young man has to say. This group is so focused that when Jesus' extended family and friends leave later that week for Nazareth, the boy gets left behind and no one notices for a day or two. Not the rabbis, not the family and certainly not Jesus. He was having just too much fun.

Well, eventually Mary notices and the family returns to the Temple and Joseph metaphorically grabs him by the ear dragging him outside to continue the two day trip back home to Nazareth. It is interesting that at least two Gospels have briefly noted that Jesus' family thought he might be a little crazy and they didn't approve of him. You get the feeling he was a hand full to raise.

...The next year, when Jesus officially became a man, Joseph could 'hand him off' to the rabbis as a full member of the congregation and their responsibility. And just like parents of teens today, that year probably couldn't pass fast enough.

Jesus, the Invisible

Remember those follow the dot coloring book pages when you were a kid? You started with the first dot and carefully dragged your pencil to the second and then the third, probably with your tongue stuck out the corner of your mouth as you concentrated really hard. The outline of the mystery figure slowly unfolded. Sometimes you missed a number and had to erase several lines before you could get back on track. And then, there it was! The mystery was solved, or sort of solved. You still had to figure out what the shape was supposed to be. But as you carefully studied the lines you could see the outline of the bear, or duck, or cat that was visible, though its shape was a little jagged around the edges you had drawn. The inside of the outline, however, was still enticingly empty, calling for you to color it in any way you wished.

Snapshots of Jesus - Through the Lens of History

And so my journey into the ancient past to discover and shoot a few great snapshots of Jesus as he was back in the day is going to take a whole bunch more research. The jagged lines I am creating by studying the historical facts and feelings of the times have barely begun to create any outline at all. But, undaunted I will continue on with my research material piled high around me.

As the title to this section suggests, the real man hidden under layers of history and histrionics may still be seen only in outline. His essence may remain invisible and I will probably have to color in the details based on my own personal analysis and assumptions. Certainly, that is what the early church found itself doing. Over the centuries many of the faithful have accepted the Gospels word for word as perfect and historically accurate and perhaps that even includes you, the reader. Well, unfortunately my own historical research based on the most modern work by highly respected divinity scholars begs for a major overhaul in my understanding of what the bible says and why it says it the way it does. Not to worry, though, because for myself my faith is not challenged -- I am instead joyfully discovering my spiritual journey is just expanding.

Now, the early church and its chaotic choices is too large a topic to be covered with a simple snapshot of the disciples, the oral traditions on which the gospels were based, and the fifty to a hundred year spread between Jesus and the first written words about him. So I will leave that tantalizing research project for another day. For now, I will head back into my accumulating articles and books and follow the trail to Jesus and see what other snapshots of his past I can capture and share with you.

The Cousins John and Jesus

Let's sneak back in time and take a quick snapshot of how John, eventually known as John the Baptist, and Jesus are related. After all, John plays a significant part in the beginning of Jesus' ministry. Let's find out why that could occur.

Mary, Jesus' mom is a cousin of Elizabeth. Elizabeth is married to a Jewish priest who has responsibilities in the Temple of Jerusalem once a year, and only once in a lifetime may he receive the honor of going into the inner sanctum of the Temple. In Luke we are told he and Elizabeth are elderly. Well, that probably means they are in their mid-thirties or early forties. From where I am, that still looks youngish to me.

Now, it was in the Temple during that once in a lifetime, prestigious honor, that Elizabeth's husband learns he will become a dad. As the story goes he is actually struck dumb by this shocking news, since he and Elizabeth haven't been blessed yet with a young'n and they are 'so elderly'. For a Jewish couple not to have children is seen in the community as something dishonorable. No kids? God must think you have done something really bad to deny you this gift. However, Elizabeth is indeed pregnant. Remember, though thrilling this may be, it is still an embarrassment at their advanced ages and so, six months later, we take another snapshot to see Elizabeth basically hiding out at home during her pregnancy in shame and fear.

At this point in time, a young, unmarried, teen-aged Mary comes to visit her cousin, and boy does she have news. She has become pregnant and asks her cousin for asylum. For the next three months until John is born Mary stays with Elizabeth, both of them hiding from family and friends, as the divine blessings blossom within them.

Although the Gospels written fifty to seventy years after these events add some gloriously poetic addendums, the bottom line is that two baby boy cousins are born to moms bonded through months of dealing with judgments and snide remarks from their community. You can see why, perhaps, the details of these beginnings were prettied up during the telling over many decades.

John, just slightly older than Jesus will be an important family member, playmate and influence on Jesus as they grow into young men. So, we will need to go back once again into the past to capture a few more snapshots to see how the teen years of angst and rebellion mold these two cousins.

. . . For now we will leave them as babies and then toddlers, and as they slowly stretching into adolescence.

Still willing to go exploring?

As the months unfolded and I shared more and more snapshots of Jesus through the lens of history in my blog, all sorts of buttons have been pushed out there in cyberspace -emotional buttons on you my friends as well as those who have stumbled across these articles in my website and probably now in this book. Receiving your emails is so interesting, uplifting and a lot of fun. I love seeing how all of you respond to history's view of Jesus.

I have to remind myself of my earlier comments from one of the first of these articles: "Breathless, but still undaunted I make the commitment to continue. I shall don my suit of personal "body armor"—an open mind, the willingness to learn, to be wrong, to be disappointed and yes, to even be amazed!"

How about you? Now that you have read this far, are you still willing to explore with me and be perhaps wrong, to be disappointed and yes to even be amazed? This is perhaps my real goal, as well as challenge in life, to break away from the ruts of ingrained thinking. And wow, some of my newest ruts came from my attempt to be non conformist not so long ago! Boy, what a surprisingly messy job this has become. From the traditional view of Jesus, to the mystical and New Age, and now to delve into the scholar's view of history, I continue on a whole new journey rife with questions and sometimes really uncomfortable answers. But, it is fun!

Well, just look at the snapshots! This is what the cousins John and Jesus were going through in their teens and then again as they grew into dissident prophets and sages. If we take a few more snapshots we will see them both questioning, and being personally challenged by their conservative upbringing, the need for political change volcanically erupting around them, and the commitment to religious truth. Notice how John ended up out in the desert emulating past prophets in his actions and attire. But wait! That will be another snapshot for the future. And then there will be even more snapshots of Jesus as he too, begins his religious quest and ministry.

. . . Time to go clean my camera lens once more.

Teenage Rebels Finding a Cause - John and Jesus

Teens tend to hang together. Friends offer the best place to air growing angst with just about everything. Nature plans this carefully so that each generation gets the chance to crave change and strive to evolve to a higher and better life. If you are a parent of a teen, perhaps seeing it this way can be a comfort. And then again, nothing usually helps except enough time for maturity to rear its long awaited self. Nothing was different for Jesus, John and their families.

Let's start the snapshots at this point with the teen John, the slightly older by six months, and his cousin Jesus. Their moms had spent emotional pregnancies together and the families probably lived in the same or nearby villages, visiting often and certainly at holiday times. This extended family would travel together each year to the

Passover celebration at the Temple in Jerusalem. The boys, also, would have come of religious age at twelve in the same year, having both studied intensely the same information in the same way. Their experiences up to now would overlap and be distinctly similar.

Now that they have become teens, what might be the obvious and not so obvious points where life begins to rub them the wrong way? How will each of them respond and act out? For now, let's begin by looking at John. Zooming in the camera a little we notice that John's dad is a priest in the local synagogue and serves frequently in the Temple at Jerusalem. Being a priest is hereditary and John would be expected to follow in his father's conservative footsteps.

Here's a quick political snapshot we will explore more fully later. The high priests in the Temple at Jerusalem were collaborators with Rome. They helped keep the peace between Jews and Roman soldiers – a thankless and much distrusted position. Remember, this was a turbulent time of insurrection. We will catch up on the importance of all this later. But for now we can immediately see the result in recorded history. John must have heatedly rebelled and said, no way! because he became a dissident, and we can catch a quick snapshot of him out in the wilds preaching about apocalyptic end times. He was becoming a strident political radical. His dad and mom must have been shocked and really ticked off.

For now, however, we will leave John eating locusts until we can travel back and take more snapshots. Then we can explore more fully his influential ministry and the profound impact his apocalyptic vision will have on his cousin, Jesus and how Jesus changes the message with his personal vision.

. . . For these two teens however, this is just the beginning of their idealistic dreams of changing the world.

PART II

The Work Begins

John, the Prophet of Doom

Before Jesus there was John. Though he was just a few months older, Jesus' cousin was super influential. Notice the amount of inches the gospel writers devoted to his story. He is also immortalized by Josephus, the Jewish historian. And in fact there are more recorded accounts about John by the non-Christian historians of the times, than there are about Jesus.

When Jesus was ready to begin his own ministry John was already well known by the people as well as the powers that be. So, let's get our camera gear and back track in time for just a few more snapshots of John the Baptist. Let's explore what was so special about this guy.

We can catch a shot of him in the 'wilderness', which is actually not that far from anywhere else. He has decided to live off the 'grid' of civilization near the Jordan River. Think 'hippie' for the moment. He has chosen his clothing very carefully for maximum impact on his audience. His hair is long and probably unkempt. His body is covered not by the tunic and over mantle worn my most, but by camel skin caught by a leather belt. This is a specific statement. This is the costume of an Old Testament prophet. John was purposefully styling himself as a 'present day' prophet and his clothes and message were in your face strident.

"The end is really, really near. Any moment God's wrath will strike down our oppressors (label them Romans) and those who sin. Then the purity of God's Law will be restored. So you had better be ready, now!" This was John's message and he screamed it loud, often and flamboyantly. He was especially critical of Herod Antipas and because of this paid the ultimate price. Herod had him arrested, imprisoned and when John still kept up the harangue he 'cut off his head'. Well, we don't actually know that part historically, but John was executed.

John prophesized impending doom. He was an 'apocalyptic prophet' and one of many that were running around the desert at that time. He was simply the most stridently obvious and well known. Jesus was his cousin and deeply affected by his message and methods. So we will have to return again to see just how Jesus' baptism by John and Jesus' blossoming ministry take an important turn after John's death.

Baptism, Purity and the 'Morning Dippers'

How often do you bath? NO, I don't really want to know. But, think about all the commercials for shampoo, bath gels, bubbles and water softeners. One would think we are obsessed with cleanliness, and one would be correct. Well, in the first century the same could be said for the ancient world. Romans had their public and private baths where the social and political occurred. The Jewish communities had their own rituals around bathing and they were quite strict and always associated with purity. So, let's travel back and catch a few snapshots of the roots of baptism, the seemingly unique activity that John offered by the Jordan River.

Set the camera for the Temple in Jerusalem. No one can enter without first ritually cleansing him or herself. The Jewish tradition was clear – if you bring uncleanness before God, God leaves! So, if you want to pray and be in the presence of the Lord you needed to be squeaky clean. And the tubs used for these rituals were at least 60 gallons and deep enough for complete submersion. There were at least 280 synagogues in Jerusalem alone and priests needed to bath three times a day. And we can see the average Jew cleansing hands and feet and perhaps bodies before each meal, before daily prayer time, before entering the synagogue, etc. etc. These were a clean people! And the purpose was for religious purity.

Let's open the lens wide and look at the wilderness. Over there we see the Essenes in small closed communities splashing that water around. Over here we see another group called the 'Morning Dippers' keeping purity before God their priority through baptism. And then, at the edge of the River Jordan, before we see him, we can hear the strident message of John. "God is coming any second to end our oppression! Are you ready? Prepare by bathing now, because when God shows up and you are not clean and pure, He will split and never set us free!"

The Gospel writers put great emphasis on Jesus coming to John to be baptized. We may never truly know why he did, but we do know that bathing ritually was a daily and very common practice for any Jew. John's uniqueness was his politically radical message. He was expecting God to come and get rid of the Romans, possibly the next minute, thereby bringing back 'old time religion' for the Jews. At this point we may catch snapshots of Jesus exploring the different religious and political Jewish sects around the area. This included his cousin John who was just one of many. We will take some good snapshots of those groups soon. Then Jesus will begin his own ministry, and we'll watch how he spins off in a completely different direction.

So, to paraphrase a contemporary Hollywood figure, "We'll be baaack!"

The Political Minefield Jesus Enters

Snapshots of Jesus - Through the Lens of History

Most Christian upbringing, just like mine, tends to create a scenario of Jesus meandering through a pink hazed landscape inside a bubble of lovely stories that insulate the reader of the New Testament from reality. We have pictured a gentle man sitting on a grassy knoll quietly sharing stories with groups of avidly interested listeners. They lean forward toward him and smile sweetly to their neighbors, while perhaps singing a first century version of 'kumbaya'. Not so! Jesus may have been inherently gentle and compassionate, but the people around him were noisy, argumentative, demanding and sometimes downright ornery. And they had reason to be that way. Let's take a few snapshots of the upheavals and hostility that surrounded Jesus as he started his ministry. The camera view will help clarify the tensions and political/religious fractures that Jesus had to deal with constantly. And it wasn't a pretty sight. The turmoil ultimately killed his cousin, forced Jesus to stay away from large cities for his own safety, and eventually led to his own crucifixion.

Keeping the history lesson short and sweet, here are a few quick photos that show the political 'mines' being placed in the field.

1000 B.C. A small tribe begins a nation and Solomon, the first king builds the Temple - the holy place where 'God can reach down and touch earth'.

600 B.C. Raiders crisscross the area and Babylonians outright destroy the Temple.

500 B.C. The Temple is rebuilt as well as the fledgling nation under Persian rule.

300 B.C Alexander the Great rides into town and wants to set up his statue inside the Temple – the Temple narrowly missed being destroyed again.

The Greeks remain, however and the Ptolomies and then the Seleucids rule. The rich Jews love the new culture and become copycats. The working class grumbles and wants a return to 'old time religion and politics'. And then, horrors of horrors the Greeks outlaw circumcision, which marks Jews as Jews, and actually erect a statue of Zeus in the Temple. Chaos reigns. The Maccabeans eventually return the nation to the Jews, but they just can't seem to stop the infighting.

63 B.C. The Romans enter the photo and create a form of stability through oppression. And guess who they name client king? The Roman pet who just loves to grovel. . . .wait for it! . . Herod the Great, now named 'King of the Jews'!

. . .And into this constantly exploding minefield walks Jesus.

The Good, the Bad and the Ugly:

Essenes, Sadducees, Pharisees, Zealots and

Bandits

Snapshots of Jesus - Through the Lens of History

A quick review of our photos shows that for the last two hundred years Jews have been obsessed with the growing belief that God was going to have to clean up the political oppression and torments visited upon them. The first great Temple had been destroyed and this was not to be forgotten or forgiven. Though the present Jewish client king, Herod Antipas renovated the second Temple bigger and better, he kept sabotaging his efforts through cruelty and love for all Roman. Bad move. Since Jews weren't able to accomplish it themselves they began asking for God to do the deed and bring an end to the outrage. Added to this, like a first century TV show of 'Survivor', there was also no end to prophets, followers and their crazy, violent schemes all hoping to end the oppression and win, with or without God. So, let's grab our cameras and zip back to the first century and record the major sectarian groups that had to have influenced, for good or for bad, Jesus and his ministry. Just as the title above announces, several groups could be found stomping, raging, sermonizing, robbing, pillaging and some just trying to escape it all. Here are a few to capture on camera, each one leaving its mark on Jesus, his ministry, his disciples and his listeners, creating personal agendas for each.

Jerusalem was a showplace and the Temple complex was an immense tourist attraction, one of the more famous in the whole world. Lots of money was coming and going and bandits were a real and violent problem. Several are noted by name by Josephus. We also can see the Sadducees, the monied Jews with noses in the air, who were ultra conservative and pro-Roman. Judaism in the first century had a fluid philosophy, but the Sadducees refused to adjust their religious views to the times and staunchly backed the oppressor. A double whammy. Then we have the Pharisees who were just beginning to relax religious standards and views but were terribly pompous about it all.

But wait, there's more. Those who hated the Romans with political venom and would eventually lead the country into political destruction by 70 A.D. were the Zealots. Note that one of Jesus' disciples was named Simon the Zealot, a hint at how diversified the personal agendas were for each disciple. Later we will explore the pressures they put on Jesus to be as they each desired. And then later we will explore how those desires colored the early church.

The most well known group was the Essenes. After thousands of years, fate and great weather conditions have given us the Dead Sea Scrolls and an extensive look into this reclusive group. Did they influence John the Baptist? Did they influence Jesus? I know I am interested!

... So, let's take a rest for now so I can do some research and then we will be back to take some great new snapshots.

Apocalypse Now!

Prophecy? Policy? . . .should I prepare?

Not too long ago the Mayan calendar came to a screeching halt. Newscasters to TV comedians, to end day survivalists were ready respectively with comments, jokes and plenty of stored water and food. Along with the dried food and automatic weapons was the grim determination that the end of the world would go out with a cosmic fireworks display. Only those who were prepared with supplies and/or great faith would survive.

Most think the idea of an end day's apocalypse came with the message of Jesus and the New Testament. Well, actually this concept was well entrenched hundreds of years before Jesus was even born. Jews were looking for an end to those pesky oppressors who kept invading their country and interfering with their religion. They wanted and demanded from God a political activist both verbal and violent to lead the war effort and remove all invaders. Enter the Zealots. They wanted and were ready for war, their kind of war, a traditional but explosively successful war.

Let's take our cameras into the fray and like all good war journalists not just follow the action, but capture the story in the faces around us.

Over there we find a strident prophet, or possibly even a Pharisee or Sadducee, revving up the already high pitched energy of groups of young men just itching for a fight and to kick some Roman and gentile butt. Groups like this are filled with that righteous sense of revenge and the need to destroy. Their vision of the apocalypse is political, religious, violent, and includes complete annihilation of the enemy. The good (read that as their own sectarian group of Jews) would be backed by God and prevail over everyone else, and they meant *everyone* else. The end days of political and religious oppression would bring back a golden age.

But, then, over here are other groups. They are philosophically and emotionally different. One of them, the Essenes, has recorded their view of the end times in the Dead Sea Scrolls, specifically the War Scroll. Summarized it says God will send his angels to help the Sons of Light (only the Essenes) destroy the Sons of Darkness (everyone else in the world including other Jews). The Essenes just have to sit back and watch. The scroll also adds that the dead will be resurrected and God's kingdom will reign on earth and heaven.

When looking at our snapshots, John the Baptist, we notice, was an apocalyptic prophet expecting the violence of war and proclaiming the need for a clean mind and body before God's imminent end days. Was he an Essene, or a political revolutionary? Or was he, perhaps, a little of both.

Still missing from our album, however, are the snapshots of Jesus and the viewpoint he would express. Be patient. He will spin off in a totally new direction and become a different and unforgettable prophet. Be prepared, he will soon appear for a photo shoot . . .but not just yet.

There are a few more snapshots to take of the first century. Our album is still unfolding.

The Dead Sea Scrolls and the Essenes

Snapshots of Jesus - Through the Lens of History

Through the mists of time come the seething, roiling, blackening clouds of political unrest. Cumulous fill with the voices of rage, pleading and simple disgust. A small group of Jews gathers itself and leaves the ancient city life of Jerusalem. They have had it! And don't want to take it anymore! So don your desert survival gear, grab your camera and let's go back to the first century. We are traveling into the wilderness – wild and wooly and really dry – but just twenty or so miles from Jerusalem. We are going to the caves of Qumran and the monastic group named the Essenes. Look up from the Dead Sea and you will see about a thousand feet above you, in the cliffs, cave openings. Take a quick snapshot and then climb. As we enter a few of the more than twenty caves we notice something striking right off the bat. There are only men, boys, and no women. Hmmm.

An elite, communal group of ultra conservative Jews have chosen to pool most if not all their personal wealth and live apart as priests. They are the righteous. They are the chosen. They are the favored by God because they are the only ones who know His will and follow it punctiliously. (I know. I know. You have probably heard this claim before by other groups, but there you go.) These Essenes are so sure of their purity they even create a different calendar, rituals and begin some interesting concepts never considered in Judaism before, like resurrection for the righteous. And they also believe in three, count them three messiahs! (We will take snapshots of the whole messiah business soon.)

Aim your camera more closely and you will see the group diligently copying the Old Testament. These men are scribes, copying the old and adding new commentaries with their own slant on Judaism. Scrolls fill jars and tables. They are also preparing for a war between the Sons of Light (the Essenes) and the Sons of Darkness (a huge conglomerate of everyone else including other Jewish sects).

The cataclysmic conflagration between cosmic forces of good and evil will continue through seven horrific battles, and is described in bloody detail in the War Scroll. Of course, they believe the end of evil times occurs when God comes to protect the elite Essenes who will then return Judaism to the mythical golden days of David and Solomon.

For more than two hundred years before Jesus their disgust grew. But it was Herod and his antics that were the final straw sending them packing into the desert. Temple politics, the defilement of values, and the worldliness of Greeks and Romans became just too gross. So they left and prayed for an apocalypse!

Now this is a really cool aside: In case you are interested, they have carefully prepared a special scroll of thin copper incised with the places where they have hidden their riches and wealth. A treasure map!

Was Jesus, or his cousin John, Essenes? Well, they certainly knew of them, and signs suggest they were familiar with all the many and diverse disputing Jewish sects. However, there were even more influences, strange and foreign, that surrounded Jesus every day.

We will need to come back with our cameras to check those out. So be prepared!

Did Jesus go to India and Tibet?

Mystical books on the mystery and magic of the East fueled the imagination of a few generations of New Age devotees. Many voiced their shared belief: Jesus must have traveled into India and Tibet. How else could his teachings sound so modern, metaphysical and hip? So let's travel back once more and take a few snapshots of the spiritual 'Happenings' that were 'socking it to' the first century.

Let's back track a bit. In 1000 B.C. King Solomon built a nation and searched for treasure from wherever he could send troops and ships. Solomon's ships sailed the coast of Africa, India and even further east to where no Jew had gone before. Since the Hindu religion is one of the oldest recorded, then first contact was probably made way back then. Jews became familiar with Hindu philosophy and it is interestingly to note they have some similarities.

In approximately 400 B.C. Buddha questions his princely upbringing and Hindu religion, wanders around, finally sits under a tree and becomes enlightened. His followers begin a new religion. Over the next few hundred years, Buddhism aggressively spreads its message mostly east to China, but also at least as far west as Parthia (Turkey and Syria), just a short hop north from the Galilee. Now, Buddhism infiltrates the consciousness of the Jewish nation.

In early 300 B.C. Alexander the Great brilliantly storms around the Mediterranean leaving his heavy handed influence everywhere. He ends with a final thrust into India where his exhausted men strike and force him to return to Macedonia and Greece. Now, this next piece of info deserves a photo op. Before he leaves he has married an Indian princess, taken to wearing local clothing and brings a Hindu guru/sage back home with him. In fact, the sage walks willingly and painlessly into his funeral pyre while Alexander and the troops watch in awe and disbelief. The influence of India has seeped into the fabric of Greece and Greek spreads through the Greek language used around the known world.

Let's also take a snapshot of the Silk Road that for hundreds of years snaked back and forth to China, and ran through India into the Mediterranean area - think first century Los Angeles rush hour. Now just a little east this thoroughfare passes directly through the Galilee to Jerusalem and beyond bringing Oriental medicine and metaphysics with it.

Gurus and Indian fakirs on beds of nails, Buddhist priests and Chinese merchants – all passed through the thriving and very Hellenized metropolis of Sepphoris, the Jewel of the Galilee.

And remember, this was only walking distance from Nazareth. Joseph and all his sons probably practiced their artisanship for the rich and snooty in the burgeoning "Jewel".

So the question remains: Did Jesus travel to India and Tibet? May be he did, but probably he didn't. He was busy growing up in a Jewish culture, learning his religion and being a good oldest son with family responsibilities until he was at least eighteen. He certainly had enough fascinating Jewish political and religious characters all around to watch and learn from.

...So, he may not have gone to the Far East, but by the first century the East had come to him with all its mystery, magic and seductive philosophies on enlightenment, making its practices and ideas hard to ignore.

Abracadabra, Jesus and Kabbalah

What is it that draws you to this robed figure of the first century named Yeshua ben Joseph, or better known to us as Jesus? Do the tales of his humble birth twang the old heart strings? Do you resonate to his simple parables about the common man? Does the vision of his muscular attack on the tables of the moneylenders in the Temple stir up your inner juices? Or, like me, are you drawn to something unknown and perhaps even unnamed – something I can only explain as his mystical other worldliness? Where could he have gained this glow, this radiance? Was he born with it? Did he study it? Was it given to him? Or was it all of the above?

You may already believe in one of the choices. For me, however, I am donning my traveling gear to see how much I can discover in the actual history of the times. What I uncover I will add to and enrich my own inner experiences of Jesus. Want to come along? O.K. then, here we go.

Every religion has its mystical branch, secretly horded and miserly shared with just a very special chosen few. In the first century we go archeological hunting for the signs of Jewish mysticism, known as Kabbalah. And yes, there it is. For hundreds and hundreds of years the mystical tradition in Judaism has grown expanding the concept of one God Whose Great Sacred Presence unfolds into the world from something that' isn't this and isn't that'.

To help understand this profound experience and process, an elaborate schematic of circles connected by lines became formalized into the 'Tree of Life'. Circles and lines were given Hebrew letters and numbers, which is where the phrase 'abracacabra' originated. By meditating for years on this Tree, contemplating the aspects of life (circles) and observing the pathways from each aspect to another (lines) you can learn the secret map everyone will need to travel to reach the Great Unknown, the greatest mystery, God.

During the first century Jesus surely knew of Kabbalah. He clearly had deep mystical experiences that probably started even in childhood. He was gifted and noticed by the elders when he was eleven. He might very well have been chosen to study the sacred and secret as a young man. The only way we may be able to guess at his possible mystical studies is to go back in time once more and delve into his message and his deeds. So let's follow the crowds, sit on the hillside and share a torn piece of bread and cooked fish, so we can bring home a few snapshots of him actually teaching and healing. And if we are respectful, we may even kneel with him as he prays and goes into his deep and sacred meditations.

I am rubbing my hands in anticipation. We will soon be following Jesus himself.

Time for Intention

How many times have you jumped into something without thinking about it first? Just jumped and saw how it all shook out? Well, we could do just that as we head back into the first century to get as close as we can to Jesus. But, I can't help feeling I need to set a very clear intention at this point. If I am not totally and completely clear on how to research this amazing individual, I will add more than I should, or leave out some things that are vitally important. So, please join me as I lay out the clearest intention and plan for follow through that I can as we begin our search for Jesus.

So, let's circle our chairs in the photography studio and start the process of setting intention.

My intention is to stay true to the title: "Snapshots of Jesus Through the Lens of History". Well, that sounds simple. But, is it? From early childhood, Jesus has been an important part of my life. When I was only about seven years old, my sister was forced to drag me out of Sunday school on Good Friday. Our minister was telling us all about the crucifixion. I was shattered by the story. I could feel the terror, the pain, the dark emotions that swirled around that cross. Emotionally, I was there! My sobbing irritated the minister no end, and I was told to leave. He just didn't understand.

Time moves on and later as an adult I had a dream of Jesus standing, smiling behind my father and mother. I woke up puzzled. By this time I had rejected the church and was at loose ends, religiously speaking. Why did he show up in my dream? However, less than a week later 'A Course in Miracles', purportedly sent by him to this century was in my hands and I gobbled it up, studying and then teaching it for the next thirty years. I felt his presence close to me.

I mention this, because probably like you, I have had my share of inner, spiritual, hard to explain experiences. For me, that has led me to write several books based on my own mystical experiences with Jesus. Well, that is ***not*** what 'Snapshots' is about. Now, the focus is on history, wherever I can find valid, well researched sources. I want to understand the times, the politics, the religious atmosphere and the people orbiting Jesus. I want to discover which parts of the bible are reliable and which have been fabricated. And yes, much of it has been by well meaning followers of the Jesus movement, right from the get go. I want to discover what he actually said back then, as best I can.

So, we will be traveling back once more to get as close as possible to Jesus, himself. As I research deeply, we will share together this truly humble rebel and miraculous healer. We will see Jesus as clearly as we can. . . through the lens of history.

Will the real Jesus please stand up?

Snapshots of Jesus - Through the Lens of History

Remember those infinity mirrors? When you looked within you saw the same reflection receding back, smaller and smaller and smaller. That's what it's like trying to find the real Jesus in the New Testament. Just when you think you catch a glimpse of him, he seems to multiply and recede further and further into the distance. Why is this?

Well, nobody actually followed Jesus around with a steno pad taking notes. All we know of him comes from oral tradition. The earliest written record was scribbled at least 20 – 30 years after his death and most scratched onto scraped hides a full hundred to a hundred fifty years later. The average telephone game gets tricky after only the third or fourth person in the circle. Image a fifty to a hundred year gap – major distortions!

So how can we discover the real Jesus? I have to admit this is not something I can do all by myself. I will have to rely on those who have gone before, the bible historians – those who have, to the best of their ability, placed their preferences aside and stuck to the facts, m'am, just the facts. Here are some of the tricks of the trade used in sifting through the ancient material.

1. "Christian" references (Christos was a Greek title added much later after his death), innuendos, events suggested before they actually happened – all these and more are clear fictions added later by the followers of Jesus. They meant well, but these are the spin doctors at work adding what they wanted Jesus to have said and done based on their political and emotional needs of those future times.

2. Quotes from the Old Testament placed in Jesus' mouth that are unlike Jesus' point of view – Jesus taught using what was

stated over and over as 'his own authority'. He clearly respected the religion of his upbringing, but rejected and was rebellious about much of Jewish tradition. He was his own man, with his own, unique and mystical viewpoint that often differed from other rabbinical experts.

3. His style was humble, offering open ended stories and ideas where people had to come to their own conclusions. He often used a turn of phrase that had you guessing and laughing. He was not pompous, high handed and strident, but immensely likable.

These three points will give you an idea of how the sifting is done. Well, that gives us a starting point. And how much of the New Testament is historically accurate and represents the real Jesus? – not a heck of a lot since so much of it represents the distorted view of those who weren't there back then and just didn't really know. . .

. . . But Jesus can be found, and we will head back in time to catch a few snapshots that will ring true and that we can keep, to hold close to our hearts.

The Temptations

Why would the gospel writers, who wanted so desperately to show the glory of Jesus, put in what can only be described as his weaknesses? They must have had a good reason. To find a possible answer we must let the past call to us once more. So, into the first century, to the edge of the River Jordan we head. Jesus has been baptized by his cousin John, the strident, apocalyptic prophet. John is soon to be arrested by Herod and then executed. John's followers, as well as his cousin Jesus are devastated by the news. Jesus is recorded as emotionally describing John as the highest and the best, clearly feeling the loss of his cousin.

As we tip toe behind Jesus, we can only guess that Jesus must be feeling his own calling stirring and grabbing him by the front of his tunic, dragging him forward. His world has turned upside down. He realizes he must be the one to continue what his cousin began. Plus, John's disciples are ready to follow John's cousin. Jesus seemed to them to be the obvious next prophet.

Get your cameras quietly ready. This is the moment we have been waiting for. Jesus feels something that wells upward from the deepest, most emotional center of his self. His own intentions must be set. He will go his own way, though John's followers will tag along not yet understanding this will be a new direction. And so, Jesus feels the need for solitude and deep reflection. Let us quietly follow him into the wilderness.

Historically, the idea of Jesus heading into a wilderness for 40 days is one of those lovely fictives that bible writers enjoy adding, laced with the poetic picture of the devil and angels. We can correctly assume, though, that Jesus shared with his disciples the struggle he did face in coming to grips with his newborn ministry. The gospel writers made sure their readers got this message loud and clear, right from the beginning: Jesus struggled with this new role. What did God want him to do and say? How did God want him to use the obvious metaphysical powers he already had manifested? Could he use his brains, his energy, his understanding of scripture, his spiritual radiance only for God's work? Was he truly up to the task? These are the types of questions that he clearly needed to contemplate and on which to pray for guidance.

And so the gospels tell us that Jesus had a deep need to pray for insight and strength. Again and again, the writers show Jesus heading out alone for long periods of time. In fact, the writers also show that the disciples were rarely sensitive to Jesus' need and intruded when they shouldn't, and then weren't there when he asked them to be. But, for now we leave Jesus pondering his future and struggling to listen carefully to God's divine guidance. His time had come.

How do you define Messiah? Ha! You'd be surprised.

Snapshots of Jesus - Through the Lens of History

Remember the movie with John Travolta when he played the angel Michael? In one scene, as he sat in the kitchen scoffing down sugar, smoking a cigarette, wearing shabby underwear, he is asked something like this, "Aren't angels supposed wear brilliant white clothes doing and saying pure things?" Without looking up Travolta, as angel Michael replies, "I'm not that kind of angel."

Keep that image in mind as we take our photo gear and travel back into a gathering of the disciples as they ask Jesus a question, not too different from the one asked above. "Are you the messiah?" they ask. And the gospel writers make note that this is asked again and again. I have to assume, all those disciples, each with a different political and religious agenda, must not have liked or understood his answer the first, second or third time they asked. Jesus, though, always answered, "Those are your words." Jesus' reply is his typical style of throwing the query right back into the questioners lap. In order to get some insight we will have to take a look at what first century Jews thought a messiah was, and what a messiah was supposed to accomplish.

When we check our photo album we have lots of shots of angry, sulky, and really violent Jews writhing against the constant oppression of outsiders ruling their country. For hundreds of years they have prayed for someone to come and chase the oppressors off and restore the best of the old times. This would be their messiah and he was seen either as politically savvy, a mighty warrior, a religious priest, or all three rolled up in one. Then God would do the rest of the saving. The Essenes wrote that they were expecting three, count them, three different messiahs that fit the above bill. This might be why Jesus was not answering that annoying question from his disciples. He knew he was not what they believed a messiah to be. He wasn't a politician. He wasn't a soldier warrior, and he wasn't interested in being high priest in the Temple.

When we travel forward in time, going past Jesus' ministry to 70 A.D., something horrific occurs to Judaism. The Temple is destroyed by the Romans. All Jews at this tragic point in time, no matter their sect, Sadducees, Pharisees, or Jesus followers who, remember, thought of themselves as Jews, no longer had the Temple to glue their identity as Jews together. This caused each of the so many differing sects to reinvent themselves, leading to some of the greatest Jewish writings being created - including the gospels.

By 100 A.D., the extremely long chain of oral tradition, just like the telephone game, was reinventing Jesus over and over again by each of the diverse sects of followers of Jesus. Keep in mind that there was not one cohesive group of early Christians. Oh no. We can take quick snapshots of a dozen or more Jewish groups who interpreted Jesus, his ministry and his death, each in their own way.

The oral traditions of all these different sects of Jesus followers morphed as they were told and then finally written down, now reflecting their many styles, needs, prejudices and aspirations leading to a whole plethora of gospels. But, only a few of these amazing gospels were chosen in 300 A. D. to be in the New Testament. . .

. . . Jesus was no longer remembered as just a humble healer and a brilliant teacher/rabbi. He was becoming a complex conglomerate of philosophies. . .

. . The gospels were creating someone and something different and unique.

Jesus and His Handlers

Snapshots of Jesus - Through the Lens of History

Years ago a friend handed me a photocopy of that famous painting of a red haired Jesus, on his knees, hands clasped, looking upward to Heaven with an imploring gaze. Underneath he had added the following caption: "Father, I know I volunteered for this assignment, but they are so dumb, dumb, dumb!" I have a feeling Jesus just may have said something just like this in Aramaic, and he was probably referring to his disciples. Some were family, some were previous disciples of John the Baptist, Jesus' deceased cousin, and all misunderstood Jesus.

His family was recorded as believing he was crazy and weird. When he was asked to come home, be with family and accept the required family obligations, Jesus replied that those who were listening to his talk and following him were his family. A lovely philosophy, but a slap in the face to his biological family standing outside the hall. The cousins that chose to be his disciples must have been seen by the family as weird outsiders, also. They had to expect a lot from Jesus to make up for their decision to rebel from family expectations.

John's ex-disciples who chose to turn to Jesus, were expecting another apocalyptic prophet. The gospels pretty consistently show them questioning and just not 'getting it'. These were politically involved rebels expecting the world to self-destruct any moment and looking for a messiah to appear - that soldier to lead the battle against oppressors, and /or the high priest to re-establish the 'correct' Judaism in the Temple.

Jesus' frustrations came right through the gospel writings. After all, these were the men who were his closest students, confidantes, and arrangers of where he taught and where he stayed.

They brought people to him, and then they jealously kept others away, especially children. These were his disciples who he depended on.

These were his handlers. . .And they just never really understood him.

Radical and Beyond

So grab your cameras as we go back to the first century and slip quietly into the house where Jesus is staying as a guest of one of his followers, probably a hated tax collector. We notice some really odd, and for the times, really shocking behavior. Jesus is not eating kosher, has not washed ritualistically as expected. He is surrounded by not just his disciples, but also women, many who are not part of his family or his hosts' family. What's going on here?

Jesus started out with a solid Jewish upbringing. We know he later hung out with his cousin John, the apocalyptic Prophet of Doom, preparing followers through baptisms, and then beheaded for his political views. Jesus clearly went from conservative childhood to radical young adult. But now, he is beginning to create his own style, his own statement. He has begun his own ministry, no longer a continuation of someone else's. He has begun to break the rules. He no longer believes the rules are what is important, but instead the content of your heart.

And what's with those women? Jewish women are respected but have their place. And here they are doing for Jesus and his disciples what men just don't do for themselves – they are cooking and serving meals to the men, as well as keeping their garments clean. And you just know they are sharing out loud their own thoughts and opinions, too.

A note about these women: They are probably expected to be respectably home with their own families, and not out gallivanting through the country; they have chosen to follow Jesus. You have to believe the ultra conservative Jews, like the Sadducees and the Temple priests, see these women as having questionable morals.

You just know they must have been called names, and you can guess what kind...

    ... So, take a lot of photos. We are now catching a good view of Jesus - the free spirit who is flaunting authority and the rules...And just begging for trouble.

'Saturday Night Live' with Jesus on the Mountain

When was the last time you sat in a really long lecture without falling asleep? I bet the ones that were the most memorable were the ones with really great speakers. So, let's take not just our cameras, but for sure our recording equipment and head back to the Galilee and attend one of Jesus' talks.

As we shuffle through a dusty road and begin to climb into the rocks along the edge of the Sea of Galilee, we can hear the talking and laughing of a large group of people. We now see them spreading blankets and pillows on the ground and on large flat rocks that form a natural amphitheater with great acoustics. In the center of the 'U' shaped area stands a man surrounded by a few others who are waving their arms and directing the arriving audience so that as many as possible will be able to hear and see. Though we see a cross section of the population, from farmers to families to Pharisees and Roman soldiers, most are local farmers and artisans. Surprisingly, a large number of women are right in the first rows.

The crowd settles and Jesus begins to speak. We are so far back, we can't catch the exact words, but we become fascinated none the less with his style. Though his features are unclear from here, we can tell he stands straight and relaxed (or history would have recorded the abnormality). And he smiles a lot as he talks. In fact, he clearly loves telling stories with great animation and humor. Laughter fills the air. He is fascinating, entertaining, stimulating, mind stretching, and even heart stretching.

He has a twist of phrase that just doesn't fit the same old rants and sermons. This is not the in your face, better accept what I say style of the average rabbis and teachers. The gospels tell us people keep remarking, 'He speaks with his own authority'. What they mean is that he speaks from personal experience. He feels of what he speaks. He lives of what he speaks. He radiates spiritual knowledge.

All are riveted to every word and gesture. Many are comforted and nod their heads in agreement. Some argue and discuss with Jesus point by point. But there are also those who are offended. They take his criticisms about lack of faith and closed hearts personally. . .

. . .and we can see trouble brewing.

Doctor Jesus

Oh boy! Researching the healings and miracles that Jesus performed has become personally challenging. My chosen title '. . .through the Lens of History' keeps me in restricted space. I want so much to sneakily drift over the line into my own beliefs, my own experiences, my own personal faith.

If you are reading this, you too, probably have an already strong spiritual and present connection with the Master Jesus. And like me are interested, even fascinated with the idea of who he might have been and what he had done back in the day. Well, now we are going into unknown territory. Don't bother to pack your camera. This will be a different king of journey.

I have to remember what we have learned together so far – the gospel writers shared memories. And they shared these memories through hymns they sung when they got together to break bread. They strung together words and phrases that stuck in their heads after Jesus repeated them many times. They added the miracles and deeds of Jesus as a troubadour would, poetically and emotionally singing them.

These hymns were shared, group to group over fifty to a hundred years before they were ever written down. Note what I just wrote – the 'history' that is 'recorded' in the gospels was taken from poetic hymns sung repeatedly. Accuracy was not the goal, but the emotional bonding of the group and groups was the goal.

Where does that leave me?

Where does that leave you when Jesus' healing power is contemplated?

For me, I will allow the stories of his love, compassion, and yes his healing power to enter my heart.

Are they accurate?

Who really knows?

But, there in my inner most tabernacle I will allow the meaning of healing and the presence of Jesus to answer me. . .

...This is as close to Doctor Jesus I will be able to get. This may not be scholarly, but you know? – This feels right and I will find myself more than close enough.

THE LAST WEEK

Snapshots of Jesus - Through the Lens of History

The Passover Powder Keg

Turn on the T.V. or internet today, and catch a glimpse of a large Middle Eastern city, its central square teeming with young men, yelling and gesturing against the powers that be. Surrounding the angry thousands are soldiers in riot gear, guns and clubs. The slightest provocation leads to violence and bloodshed. Hold that image and come with me to Jerusalem in the first century. Grab your cameras and stay close together, the journey will be tumultuous.

We enter history during the week of Passover, the highest holiday in Judaism. Thousands are pouring into Jerusalem and squeezing into the thirty-five acre Temple complex to purchase their lambs for the family Passover dinner. As we stand to the side of the entrance gate we can't help but notice the Roman soldiers – they surround the entrance, they patrol all the streets and alleys, they are rude and menacing. As we look up, the walls of the Temple are HUGE as they rise above us. But wait, looming over the walls of the Temple is another structure! This stone walled watch tower extend along the side of this sacred Temple, glaring down with hostility and superiority. Here the Roman army stands guard commanding an unobstructed view into the most holy of ground for the Jews, the place they believe God Himself touches the Earth.

As we surreptitiously snap our cameras, notice the faces in the crowds jostling to enter the Temple grounds. They quickly glance at the soldiers and move on, then, they glance up at the abomination of the Roman tower that watches and waits. You can feel the Jewish anger and growing seeds of rebellion that will eventually explode a short twenty-five years in the future when violence results in the burning and destruction of the whole

Temple. But, for now, our cameras pick up the glowing embers of revolt in the hearts of the thousands who must practice their faith and live in their own country under the grinding hob nailed boots of the Roman soldiers.

Stay together now, as we are pushed into the Temple courtyards. We catch a glimpse of the High Priest, Ciaphas. We can almost smell the overwhelming stress he feels. The Sanhedrin, seventy priests and Jewish elders, must keep the crowds orderly and respectful of the religious Law using their own police force. The Sanhedrin must also act as go-betweens with the Roman authorities and the Jewish nation and is the only barrier between the Jews and the weight of Roman law and its repercussions. These overworked priests and elders are seen as money grabbing collaborators. Yet without their delicate political dance, chaos and bloodshed, destruction and annihilation would follow.

As we shuffle back to the streets, and move toward the entrance gate to the city, we notice a small crowd dancing and waving their arms as they follow a figure. Take some quick snapshots of that simply robed figure riding into town on a donkey for the high holiday. . . he is soon to enter the roiling masses of the sacred, and the sacrilegious mayhem . . .

... Be patient. We will be back to follow this quiet and dignified figure from the Temple to beyond.

Dinner for Thirteen, please.

Scent and smell trigger memories better than any other sense we have. Catch the scent of cut grass and you are back playing tag with your friends. The aroma of onions and celery coming from the neighbors' houses brings the vision of Thanksgiving dinner and your mouth begins to water. The sweet fragrance of a baby's soft hair triggers the thought of having another child.

Now, take a good sniff, and across centuries of time you can catch the scent of cooking fires and roasting lamb from the city of Jerusalem. It is time for the Passover meal in the first century. Let's not be late.

Quietly enter the large room where a particular Passover dinner has already begun. We find Jesus and his apostles being served by several women, clearly close friends and family members. For hundreds of years this particular dinner ceremony has been observed and includes four ritual servings of wine. Notice that Jesus leads each part of the ritual meal, explaining carefully and then personally refining each explanation.

Look closely at the attendees – some are chatting with each other, some are watching Jesus with glowing love, and there is one that sits sulky and disappointed. Jesus has not lived up to his political expectations.

Now look closely at Jesus – he is not his usual light hearted self. He seems serious, slightly subdued and, yes, somehow sad. His eyes rest on each one in the room with love and then stops for a moment on the only attendee nervous and grumpy, fidgeting in his seat. Their eyes meet – Jesus knows and understands, and the apostle knows that Jesus knows. We watch as both their hearts break, just a little.

What is actually said, we will never truly know. But, when the dinner is complete, Jesus slowly leaves. His heart is heavy and he has much to ask of God this night. . .and we will quietly return to see what the rest of this night brings.

In the Garden

A few years ago a gray cat walking behind a Buddhist monk filled one of my dreams – a 'temple' cat. The next day a sweet gray kitten adopted me at Petsmart. When I looked up gray cats (known as blues) on Google I learned they originally came to Europe with the Templar knights during the Crusades. Hmmmm…. 'templar cats?' Here was a neat example of having a mini-vision during a night's sleep. If this kind of knowing is pretty common for us mere mortals, how more so must be the knowing for someone truly masterful.

    Let's once more travel back, this time to the Mount of Olives and quietly follow the sad, troubled figure of Jesus. He has just left the Passover meal and has asked a few of the apostles that he loves most fondly to come with him. He has seen his future, as a master would. Yet, his insight into what will happen to him is not that surprising. Until recently he has pointedly stayed away from major cities and the authorities, and answered questions carefully and diplomatically. However, both the Jewish and Roman authorities keep careful watch, and though he is not the only 'troublemaker' they are worried about, he is certainly on the list of the 'most wanted'. He remembers that his cousin John, just two or three years before had been arrested and then killed, and many of Jesus' followers were John's. Jesus knew what was coming.

Consider if you knew you had only days, or only hours to live, and your ending would be not only excruciatingly painful but humiliating as well. In this state of mind, we watch Jesus trudge down into the Garden at the foot of the Mount of Olives. We see him implore his beloved apostles to pray with him to help give him strength. As the night goes on they fall asleep and Jesus struggles, and prays and struggles, all alone . . .

... But wait, we hear the stomping of feet. And into the garden come the hobnailed footed 'cops'. They have their assigned task and they do it. Jesus' fate is now sealed

Trial by Senhedrin

How many times this week did you want to advise a friend or loved one, to direct them away from destructive behavior? Were you diplomatic and gentle, or did you just have to let them know how really dumb they are? Now, did your friend or loved one accept your advice when offered? Did you need to offer your advice repeatedly? And did you get just a little huffy when your really super advise was refused?

Well, let's head back to the first century and take a look at the developing pattern of interactions Jesus had with the priests and elders, and notice the inevitable and tragic results.

In the Gospels, Jesus, is remembered as directing followers to first take an errant brother aside and privately redirect him. If that doesn't work, followers should join in a group of two or three and confront the wrong-doer. Now, if that doesn't work, the desperado should be dragged in front of the Temple elders for something stronger and more persuasive. And if that doesn't work either, send him away and treat him like a leper.

Take some quick snapshots as this same pattern plays out with Jesus and the elders. First a priest would approach Jesus and begin a debate. Later, two or three would confront him and debate with him again. When all confrontation shifted Jesus not one iota from his continued sermons at the local synagogues and on the hillsides, the next step is taken - sending the Temple guards into the Garden to bring him before the Sanhedrin, the Temple priests and elders, for a really nasty rebuke.

What happens at this emotionally charged trial is supposition, since nothing was ever recorded and no followers of Jesus attended. We do know that Jesus must have exasperated them completely since they sent him ignominiously off to the next level of authority. . .

. . .and so we will return to take snapshots at the next trial, presided over by Pontius Pilate.

Pontius Pilate – A Day at the Office

Think back to the worst job you ever had. Remember how each day was enormously depressing. Thank goodness you have moved onto something better. (Oops! Sorry if you are still in it.) Now, this is the state of mind for Pontius Pilate in the first century. He didn't ask to be a Roman procurator in this hot and volatile section of Israel, but here he is slowly dragging his feet from responsibility to responsibility. And one of the more onerous was overseeing the high Jewish holiday of Passover in the city of Jerusalem.

Now, let's snap a quick photo of Pilate's residence, the place he tries hard not to leave. He lives on the pleasant coast of Israel in the voluptuous city of Ceasarea. His villa has all the comforts of the modern first century – running water, baths, gardens and lots of servants. Yet, once every year he has to trudge over to Jerusalem and amass his troops to do crowd control for the Passover holiday. And to a Roman this ain't a pleasant assignment. During the last years, violent revolutionaries, screeching prophets, oppressed lower classes, and roving bandits have reached a crescendo and plagued his tour of duty. Pilate's form of policing and peacekeeping is swift and final – just grab 'em and crucify 'em! The bodies hanging on crosses outside the city are constantly being replenished. Take photos only if you want them in your own album.

Pilate and the High Priest of the Temple meet when necessary, which is often during this holiday week. Together they share the burden for keeping a semblance of peace in the city.

Whether a ripple of revolt or tsunami of insurrection occurs, the Sanhedrin is required to turn over any Jewish troublemaker to Pilate for quick trial and immediate penalty on the old rugged cross. Jesus was a radical and yes, seen as interfering in Temple politics, as well as a possible threat to Roman authority. The rules were the rules so inevitably Jesus had to be found guilty by the priests and given over to the Romans.

Many movies, books and myths have tried to capture the emotional climate of Pilate on the day when the priests of the Temple of Jerusalem turned Jesus over to the Romans.

What did Pilate think?

What guilt and remorse, if any, did Pilate experience?

What we do know from history, is that Pilate was simply trying to keep the peace, giving short shrift to just one more dissident, one more troublemaker. Pilate kept Jesus' trial short, the penalty just another tedious necessity in a long line of similar incidents. This was such a daily 'ho hum' activity that first century historians barely recorded this particular prisoner's trial, verdict, and inevitable penalty.

Over the next two thousand years, Jesus followers have layered more and more meaning and glory onto an event that, at the time, was seen as an almost unimportant blip on the screen - though it was crushingly sad and confusing to Jesus' family and followers. . .

...But, we will return, bringing our cameras to record as much depth and insight as possible about this amazingly short event that has none the less impacted the world for millennium.

The Crucifixion

Josephus, the still highly respected Jewish historian of the first century spent a lifetime documenting Jewish history. He covers this history in fascinating but almost excruciating detail. And yet, when he made mention of the event fifty years after the crucifixion, his comments were a really short few sentences, and an obvious echo of the standard language in Christian hymns sung at that time. This tells us something of the impact, or lack thereof, Jesus' crucifixion had on the general Jewish, Greek and Roman populace fifty years after the fact.

Today, the faithful look back two thousand years with a powerful laser beam of emotional and even fanatical interest that leads to a distorted belief that Jesus' life and death and perhaps resurrection hit the ancient world like an atomic blast: This event just couldn't have been missed. Unfortunately, that was not the case. (But, we will take a quick snapshot of the impact on the early church much later.)

For now, let's discover what the everyday crucifixion was actually like, since this is what Jesus suffered. Take photos only if you want them in your own album.

After being found guilty, the criminal was given the obligatory whipping. Humiliation followed, and for Jesus this included a thorned crown and sign above him on the cross mockingly saying , "King of the Jews". This represented his political crime since the only king of the Jews was considered the Roman emperor. The criminal then carried just the cross bar up to the hill outside of the city, since the posts were left in the ground for the daily crucifixions that occurred.

Golgotha was not a tourist attraction. This was a place people avoided. There would be few people to watch this tortuous event, perhaps only family and a few close friends. But, keep in mind. Jesus was a political criminal, and so showing support at his death tarred the supporters with the same crime. Peter understood this and denied knowing Jesus several times. Cowardly, perhaps, and painfully regretted, but understandable.

Nails were driven through the wrists, not hands, and a wedge on the post was placed in the most uncomfortable of spots, between the legs. All engineered to painfully support the weight of the criminal for the longest time possible. Most died from asphyxia as the lungs filled with fluid as did Jesus', since recorded memories tell us a sword thrust in Jesus side caused fluid to run.

After his death, the body was removed by family and given a resting place in a tomb donated by a faithful follower of the beloved rabbi.

We don't have to take any photos, we can head back to the present and see what tradition says is the actual tomb still preserved near Jerusalem. Certainly, you can get on the internet and see the photos already taken by others over the years.

What actually happens next in the story of Jesus? . . .

. . .I will research and contemplate this, and then share my discovery in the next section.

The Aftermath - Splinters

Shock! Disbelief! Denial! Anger! Questions! Trying to make sense of it all! The followers of Jesus are not just one group of apostles, but many groups scattered around the area, more than you can count on two hands – each one creating its own coping mechanism for Jesus' death.

We have gathered photos of Jesus from the beginning until the seeming end. Yet, just like the Jesus followers after the crucifixion, we need a few more answers and a clear direction. So, grab your cameras as we go back to the first century.

Take time to snap lots of photos of all the disparate groups calling themselves followers of Jesus spread around the Mediterranean, each with a different take on what happened after the crucifixion. Some are really ticked off that just a few short years after they lost John the Baptist shrieking that the end of the world was near, their next great prophet extolling a new world, has been killed. And there is still no sign of a new world.

Some followers retell the stories and parables that Jesus shared, to begin a rich source of hymns that will form the basis of the accepted gospels. Notice and take some snapshots of how some of these groups are creating a lineage of stories, each lineage reflecting the teachings of an original apostle. There is a Mark group, Matthew group, John group, Thomas group, Mary group – each singing their memories of Jesus during their weekly home meetings.

Here is an intriguing fact I discovered: The original gospel of Mark, the first to be written down a good twenty years after Jesus' death, ends not with resurrection but simply an empty tomb. It will be only decades later that stories of a resurrected Jesus will be added to the hymns and then eventually the gospels.

The Matthew and Luke gospels, written decades after the original Mark, take huge swaths of exact lines from the Mark gospel and then glue on the resurrection story. Only a very long time later is the resurrection added to the gospel of Mark.

Historian now have large and small fragments from many gospels circulated back then, and all need to be seen as just as important as the four chosen three hundred years after Jesus' death to be the only 'official' ones. Historians now agree all the gospels were created as propaganda pieces for particular groups of Jews and/or gentiles. They never were considered 'history', just memories to be handed down.

Fifty years after Jesus, the Romans finally burn down the Temple, most of Jerusalem, and the angry, heartsick Jews spread out across the world. Jews no longer have a single identity tied to the Temple in Jerusalem. Jews are a shattered and splintered people creating new and different sects - the Jesus followers become some of them – all trying desperately to recreate a new Jewish identity. By this time the original apostles, as well as a man named Paul (who took the tale of Jesus to the Gentiles), are all dead. Most killed by the Romans.

Take a snapshot, for it will be during this confusing time the name 'Christian' starts to be used. Gospels are now written and shared. . .

...Letters copied and sent around to blossoming communities around the Mediterranean...

...Christianity is born

Resurrection- A Very Private Matter

Snapshots of Jesus - Through the Lens of History

Once more I scan my self-appointed title, 'Jesus through the Lens of History'. What has history discovered about the resurrection of Jesus? What have we, together, discovered as we took snapshot, after snapshot?

The original and first gospel, Mark's, never mentioned resurrection and ended with an empty tomb. Only much later grieving followers began grappling with the death of Jesus. To find answers they went to the only place of wisdom used by Jews for centuries – the scriptures and the prophets. Here, they plumbed the eloquence of Isaiah and found the words that would both comfort and explain. A messiah would come and lead them to a new world. Jesus was this messiah.

Are the stories of Jesus' resurrection accurate or allegory? I must come to my personal conclusion. The glory and splendor told in the New Testament I will need to accept on faith. And so I ask the next obvious question - What does the resurrection of Jesus mean to me? And perhaps, you must ask this also - What does it mean to you?

I will put away my camera and close my eyes. Inside my own heart and mind will I ask for Jesus to enter . . .

Here, he is fully alive, resurrected in the spirit.

Here, I ask him to explain it all to me.

Here, I will discover the meaning of his death and his resurrection . . .

. . . and here, in my heart,

> I will melt into the loving presence of my savior.

To enjoy more books by Bette Jean Cundiff please visit:

www.miracleexperiences.blogspot.com